POEMS I DON'T HATE

TRISTA MERRILL

FAERY CAT PRESS

Poems I Don't Hate
Second edition

Copyright 2020, 2019 by Trista Merrill

eBook ISBN 978-0-9894278-4-5
Print ISBN 978-0-9894278-4-5

Cover Design
Trista Merrill

Interior Design
April Steenburgh

All rights reserved. No part of this book may be reproduced or transmitted in any form by any means, electronic, mechanical, photocopy, recording or other without the prior written permission.

To the family and friends that have stood by me through it all.

And to JDB...he knows why.

CONTENTS

April's Bones	1
Parking Lot Gulls	4
She Rescues Fish	6
The Renegade Book Club	9
Tears For Norway	11
Rain	13
Loki	15
Except It Isn't	17
Demotivational	19
Pantoum	22
Little Things	24
One Moment	27
A Story-Teller's Lament	28
The waterfall	29
Pen to Paper	31
Fog	32
Alarm	34
Renewal	36
Today	38
The invitation	39
Range	41
Sole Diving	43
Kailee	45
The Poet As Artist	46
Liminal	49
Musing	51
Silence	52
Empty Doorways	54
Dawn	56
Hell Hath No Fury	58
I am, I guess	61
Romanticizing	63
A Fleeting Darkness	66
As I lay dreaming	68

A Wolf in Hannah's Clothing	71
Bessie	73
Dachau, December 1995	75
Crazy Women	77
I am a Feminist	80
Blossoms	83
Just Moving	84
Just Students	86
Secondhand Memories, August 11, 1995	87
The Test of the Wine Taster	91
The Logophile	92
Trying Not To Dwell	94
Fenestra	96
World Of Meaning	98
About the Author	99

APRIL'S BONES

I. *Them*
    When the winter snows have finally relented
    And we see the first hints of a fresh born spring
    Rising up from the dead,
      They are there.

GLEAMING white in the rejuvenated sunlight
    Long after the muscle and flesh and sinew,
    The feathers and the fur
    They are there.

SOME ARE PERFECT, nested in leaves and moss
    Unmolested by weather, time, or teeth
    Placed as if in reverence
    They are there.

        . . .

OTHERS ARE RAGGED, discolored, broken, chipped
    Bearing the scars of a hard life and a harder death
    They gave it all and more,
    They are there.

EACH ONE TELLS the story of a life full cycle
    A harsh winter, ravaging illness, the hunter,
    Left where fallen or dragged,
    They are there.

II. You
    You are a child of the earth, vibrant and alive,
    Collecting and crafting your oddments and curiosities
    For reasons that you cannot voice,
    But they are there

THE EARTH BENEATH YOUR FEET, the trees all around,
    You walk among them as if born there,
    The hills and the gullies, the hidden waterfalls,
    They are there.

YOU LOOK for them as you walk, your eyes darting
    From whitened branch that might be, but isn't,
    You find them, drawn to their stories,
    They are there.

YOU TAKE up what once was and ever shall be
    Tracing lifetimes in hollows and rough edges
    Feeling for connections

They are there.

YOUR ANCESTORS, your sisters and brothers
    The living spirits of Mother Earth
    You smile and you know
    They are there.

PARKING LOT GULLS

The seagulls circle above the parking lot
    Crying out in plaintive disarray
    I wonder if they are looking for the sea
    But there is no sea here.

On a clear day sunlight will dance on the lake
    And we can see the shimmer from here.
    But now, the sun has only begun to rise
    And the sky is still a muted grey.

But even so, I wonder why the gulls
    Do not sweep towards the silver glass
    Where the fish in muted silence
    Swim silently in plaintive disarray

Instead they circle the parking lot
    Scanning the pavement of faded lines

Looking for a morsel of bagel or a French fry.
   Weaving intricate patterns in the early dawn

Perhaps they are not lost after all, I muse.
   For it was us who named them for the sea.
   Romanticizing their harsh call
   And their scavenger ways

But sometimes, I, too, feel misaligned
   As I fish for dreams in the barren concrete
   Crying out in plaintive disarray
   And looking for the sea.

SHE RESCUES FISH

Child safely on the bus
    Never noticing the tank
    Which seemed fishless
    No hungry fin calling

Panic.

She lifts dripping items
    One by one from the tank
    Until one hollow rock
    Has a new sound

Hope.

Not just water dripping
    But a strange flapping

As a tail fin striking
Desperate against rock

CURIOSITY.

SOMEHOW STUCK INSIDE
    A bizarre problem
    That somehow reflects
    An unusual life

MEMORY.

THIS SAME FISH once
    Sailed, waterless
    To land across a room
    Flipping much the same.

FOCUSED.

THE PROBLEM at hand
    Submerge the rock
    Peer through refraction
    To awkwardly release

TRIUMPH.

LANGUISHED SWIMMING

    Mother saved
    No lies, no tears.
    Except her own.

Relief.

One small shining deed
    Lost in the sea of the world
    But monumentally important
    To one fish, one boy.

THE RENEGADE BOOK CLUB

It has been said a thousand times in as many ways
    That the body is a canvas,
    But since I play at being a writer,
    I think of it, rather, as a blank page.
    And even as I sit to write these words
    I am thinking of a new story
    To be scrawled in living ink;
    And even as you sit to listen this,
    I can remember the pain
    Beneath the carven image.

WHEN DID YOU GET IT?
    Who did the artwork?

A RITE OF PASSAGE, a secret handshake,
    A culture diverse despite persistent images
    Of bikers, anarchists, rebels, and hippies.
    We tell these tales to one another;

Countless interpretations of the same page
For every line and shade has a story to tell,
Each bearing witness to the paths of our lives
Etched in black ink on blank skin, indelible.
There is no easy edit, no revision, no retraction,
Just the precise story mulled over for days, months.

WHAT DOES IT MEAN?
  How many do you have?

WE GATHER in corners and coffee shops,
  Doorways and offices, in stores and on streets,
  Connected by something that is different for all,
  But still binds us in blood and needles,
  Like some renegade book club.
  Talking of things that separate us from the scared,
  the disinterested, the confounded.
  I don't know what others see when they read
  This story-filled page...but like any good book club,
  It is the discussion they inspire that binds us.

WHAT WAS YOUR FIRST?
  When I got mine...

AND THE STORIES go on and on...

TEARS FOR NORWAY

Pale Nordic skin,
    Touched by raindrops
    And water from the lake.
    Shivering with gooseflesh
    Brought on by rain and fear
    Huddling in confusion

YOU SHED your clothes
    Hoping to swim away,
    But the lake drained you
    And you turned back
    Knowing that you were wading
    Into the cold jaws of hell

YOU LAY STILL, silent
    The bodies of friends
    Pressing in against you
    Crushing the panic within you

    The rain washing away
    Blood you will always feel

You could hear him
    Breathing on a rock
    His taunts and laughter
    Still in your ears
    Then the bullet came
    And you heard nothing

The world is watching
    Struggling to understand
    Why he came for the children
    Faces not Nordic, but human
    Grieving for the innocence
    Shed like clothes on a rocky beach

RAIN

The fountain is still running,
    though the day is still and heavy
    and a sullen rain drips greyness.
    The drops can barely dent or dimple
    water already gushing with movement.
    Oblivious to the rain's touch, the fountain dances.
    Rushing ever upwards,
    crashing joyfully into the pool,
    then dancing upward to play again.
    No sun highlights the hidden color of the water,
    No breeze accentuates its tumbling.
    No children dip tiny feet into refreshing pools.
    There is just clouds and rain,
    a grey sky pressing down.
    There is just drizzle, and a light fog hiding
    hiding what lies ahead, beyond, around.
    The fountain exists in a tiny space
    And yet it dances.
    The sound of water kissing water
    Creates the only music it needs.

. . .

A SILENT OBSERVER walks into this scene from the fog,
    a bowed head raising upwards to gaze
    for only a moment before falling
    to rest damp chin on cold chest.
    The figure disappears once again, all too aware of the rain
    and the greyness of the day.

AND STILL THE FOUNTAIN DANCES.

LOKI

As I write these lines, there is a spider
    Running amok somewhere on my desk.
    The cat, which was calmly on my lap,
    Is now randomly giving wild chase.
    Alas, he is having no luck against his tiny foe.
    So he returns to exuding waves of indifference.
    My evening is sporadic moments still and calm.
    Interrupted by tiny eight-legged movement
    And then a mad feline scramble
    To the random corners of my desk.

I AM GETTING no work done.
    I'm either on the watch for tiny legs
    That move in undulating creepiness,
    Or I am distracted wholly by the cat
    Who is somehow asleep and alert
    At the same time, as only cats can be.
    When he leaps towards his prey,
    His tail waves lines of obstruction

>   Blocking my sight and invariably failing
>   To catch the spider that taunts us both.

OR PERHAPS IT is merely the cat who is taunting.
>   He begs me look with him around the room,
>   Staring at random corners and empty walls.
>   His yellow eyes alert, his body poised, hunting.
>   His ears rotate to catch the tiniest sound, ready.
>   His tail lashes for a few minutes, but then…it stops.
>   It curls into stillness and his lids slide slowly close.
>   Until at last he poses for all the world like Bast-et,
>   Sitting erect as he falls into a deep feline sleep.
>   Not six inches from my face.

AND WHENEVER I try to save my drink and my work,
>   I know that I am paying for what I wrought.
>   He is a cat, and therefore the rules are his,
>   But I have compounded it by naming him for Loki,
>   At once crafty and malicious and heroic
>   Divine, empowered, full of grace,
>   Misunderstood and troublesome, a giant among gods.
>   And while I would further sing his praises,
>   I cannot, for there is a spider running rampant on my desk,
>   And a swirl of furry retribution has been unleashed.

EXCEPT IT ISN'T

I take a deep breath and hit send.
    The invitation hurtles to you,
    And within moments, you reply.
    I smile and then go about my day,
    Curious.
    It's just lunch, except it isn't.

IT SEEMS SO SIMPLE, so normal.
    A brief car ride with just two
    Side by side with no work to do.
    No text pause to collect thoughts,
    Immediate.
    It's just talk, except it isn't.

PARK, go in, order food, wait
    Find a table, sit, arrange, eat.
    Talk about work, life, cats
    Casual.

It's just a meal, except it isn't.

I DON'T SOCIAL WELL, I say,
　　You don't either, you claim
　　But oddly this is easy,
　　Comfortable.
　　It's just awkward, except it isn't.

DEMOTIVATIONAL

An electric shock jolts through my leg,
    A shudder, air sucked through my teeth,
    The pain is sudden, intense, and blinding,
    My body tries to fold in on itself, rigid
    And then just like that, it's gone.

Your body is a temple,
    the Good Book reads,
    But mine is filled with unholy fire,
    The sacred left corrupted, crumbling

I TRIED TO LOG THEM, but lost count.
    I tried to study them, but no pattern.
    In quiet moments, I try to forget them,
    In sleep, in driving, sitting, relaxing with friends.
    But they come without warning, relentless.

                  . . .

Pain is weakness leaving the body,
    The recruiter says,
    but I'm left weakened, shaken
    Afraid in and of my own skin.

The words float *into my awareness, heavy*
    Something has changed with my familiar demon
    So, MRI, steroids, perhaps more spinal injections
    We will push it through quickly if we can,
    Because it is clear you are not feeling well.

Love the body you're in.
    The motivators preach,
    But if my body does not love me?
    What then, when love brings pain?

I am *sore from tensing up in reaction,*
    Weary from the heavy weight of frustration,
    Tired from the constant worry and fear,
    Hope seems to be slipping away.
    I can see sympathy in the doctor's eyes.

Take care of your body and it will take care of you,
    The poster reads
    But mine is a battlefield, locked in combat
    And there's no retreat to safer shores.

And so *I go home and resume the wait,*
    The wait for procedures and pills,
    For questions to find answers,

For the next wave to come and then go
For whatever comes next.

T<small>AKE CARE OF YOUR BODY</small>. It's the only place you have to live
   He says, but what if I do?
   What if am a prisoner in the only body that I have?
   Because it's the only place I have to live.

PANTOUM

Telling stories of the children, little girls and little boys
    Memories of the six of them growing up after the war
    I feel a tugging at my heart with every word she speaks
    Truth and memory intertwine with dementia and disease

Memories of the six of them growing up after the war
    Some of the stories have characters that exist for none but her
    Truth and memory intertwine with dementia and disease
    She talks of things that never were and things that cannot be

Some of the stories have characters that exist for none but her
    She alone can see the children playing tricks and poking fun
    She talks of things that never were and things that cannot be
    Knowing but then forgetting that her mind is not her own

She alone can see the children playing tricks and poking fun
    She hides things to protect them so her room is somewhat bare

Knowing but then forgetting that her mind is not her own
We leave her in the little room that now must be her home

SHE HIDES things to protect them so her room is somewhat bare
    I feel a tugging at my heart with every word she speaks
    We leave her in the little room that now must be her home
    Telling stories of the children, little girls and little boys

LITTLE THINGS

He was cowering at the highest level,
    His white fur bright against the black mesh,
    He hides most of the time, shy and defensive,
    So it was strange to see him there.
    His eyes were closed.

I LOOKED CLOSER and saw that he was damp,
    As if he'd fallen into water, but there's none
    Except in a bottle that drips only when he wants it.
    His breathing seemed ragged to me.
    His eyes were closed.

I OPENED the cage and he started , then settled.
    I stroked him slowly, gently, unused to being that close.
    He sat there wheezing, damp, and unaware.
    His tiny nose quivered and my throat hitched.
    His eyes were closed.

                . . .

I slid a small box into the cage, Special K granola,
    And nudged his little feet with it, he opened one eye
    And then scrabbled into the box, moving to the corner.
    I stuffed some tissues in so that I could still see him.
    His eyes were closed.

For a day and a half I watched him, peering into
    The box, at random times of day and night waiting.
    Squinting to see him in the eerie glow of my phone,
    With bleary eyes still blinking away the recent sleep.
    His eyes were closed.

His brother, sandy and equally tiny, sometimes sat
    Crouching on the opposite corner of the box, twitching
    It felt like he was asking why it was, demanding I help.
    His dark eyes seemed to ask me to fix his brother
    Whose eyes were closed.

And then one afternoon, after a long day of errands,
    The box was empty, or, more accurately, half-shredded.
    I felt a skip in my heart, fearing the worst as I searched,
    Looking under other boxes, afraid to find his body had stiffened,
    His eyes remaining closed.

I tried to steal myself against a tiny heartbreak of sadness,
    But then, I saw what I least expected I would see,
    A tiny white face tucked behind an empty cardboard tube,
    Little white feet holding a half-eaten cracker, nose twitching,
    His eyes wide open.

                . . .

AND ME, well, my eyes grinned into his pink ones,
    As I keep going back to visit to make sure of it all.
    I wonder at how I dared overlook their importance
    In the face of fuzzy tails, tiny fingers, and sharp teeth.
    But now my eyes are open.

ONE MOMENT

At five am I quietly woke up
    With her pressed against my belly
    Her weight resting against my legs
    A ruffled pile of soft dark fur
    Curled into the hollow of my body
    Finding my lap even in my sleep
    The house was dark, still, silent
    Except her gentle breathing
    Somewhere between a purr and a rasp
    She was warm, familiar, soothing
    And I held that moment for eternity.
    It was the last time.

A STORY-TELLER'S LAMENT

I walked the earth today
    But only in thought.
    I lived the perfect day,
    But it was nighttime.
    I laughed a carefree laugh,
    But it reached not my lips.
    I loved completely today,
    But who was there to see it?
    All I have done and seen and heard
    Does not exist outside my mind.
    Ah well, tomorrow is another day
    And I am never short on dreams.

THE WATERFALL

the waterfall is alive, though it's just water
    forever cascading,
        telling the lifetimes of endless drops
        telling the stories of changing rock
        shifting over time
        and always falling, falling, falling

THE WIND SINGS to me as I stand here
    the raging tumult
        singing me into a deafening silence
        singing me into a staggering dance
        just holding on
        but still falling, falling, falling

THE MIST DRENCHES me in the cold wash
    borne on the winds
        cleansing me from the skin inward
        cleansing burdens from my shoulders

    tears drowned in mist
    but always falling, falling, falling

THE POOL in constant rhythmic motion
    explores the cavern floor
    calling me to dive deep into its depths
    calling me like a lover to its embrace
    my heart is deep in love
    and still falling, falling, falling

PEN TO PAPER

Pen to paper
    Heart to line
    Feel the rhythm
    Sound the rhyme
    Write the letter
    Craft the poem
    Sing the song
    That brings them home
    Find the voice
    To speak your mind
    Perfect phrase
    Frame a line
    Spill your heart
    In voice and word
    Ensure each thought
    Each beat is heard
    Hearts and lives
    Must intersect
    Use your words
    To each connect

FOG

A fog has rolled across the damp night,
    Casting everything in a muted lamplit haze
    Muffled, lost, embraced, and dreaming,
    Sound seems to fold in on itself in the dark.

I step outside and feel it settle on my shoulders,
    The feathered burden of a thousand raindrops
    Seeking purchase in the deep night
    I can hear nothing…not even the hint of a breeze.

The air is chill with the last vestiges of winter
    While spring dances on the edges of my senses
    Even now, in this fog-drenched night
    I can feel warm tomorrows and deep sunlight.

But for now there is only muffled silence,

The chill, damp air drenching my skin,
The dreaming fog erasing the wider world
And me, alone in this silent cocoon, waiting.

ALARM

the chirp of the defective fire alarm
    fades in and out of my consciousness
    like a badly tuned instrument
    playing the same note in a steady rhythm
    of insistent, relentless, pointless sound

I CLOSE my eyes and listen for it
    remembering back to a professor
    who once said there is no such thing as silence
    in some ways, i suppose he was right...
    but in the moment the fire alarm fades
    from my mind, he is egocentrically wrong

IF I TRY NOT to hear it, it pushes into my ears
    and if i try to hear it, it does the same thing
    like so many other things in life, it has control,
    i can only control it when i think of other things
    look what i can do... push away this reminder

that this old apartment may be slowly crumbling

THOUGHTS of a broken fire alarm lead outward
    and i think about trying to find a house
    saddened by a world where april snowstorms
    become second fiddle to dangerous violence
    erupting in some other place that isn't home,
    but could have been....may someday be

AND SO THIRTY-TWO seconds pass in silence
    silence marred only by the chirp
    of a defective fire alarm that reminds me
    in a steady bleat, that it has broken
    unable to fix it, i go on with my life
    marveling that sometimes, i can't even hear it.

RENEWAL

Fingertips touch the dancing water
    As she kneels to kiss the gentle waves
    She turns her head to let her hair float free
    Like a fiery water lily

IN A FLASH SHE DIVES, losing her self
    Surrounded completely by water
    She hears Silence and holds it to her
    A ray of light darting through the water

SHE BREAKS the surface and air kisses her lips
    The water runs from her, leaving a bright sheen,
    A coat of shining jewels clinging to her body
    She twirls and the water nudges against her thighs

HER ARMS REACH up towards the bright sky, water cascading
    tiny rivers trace her form like rain on a sunny afternoon

The song and the dance and the moment rush through her
Such energy to dry the very water from her skin,

BUT SHE ALWAYS RETURNS TO DOUSE HERSELF again
    As if to quench the very fire of the Sun
    Or set fire to the very stillness of the Moon
    Instead the two combine and there is *her*

TODAY

Today I need to be stronger.
    I need to love myself
    As well as you.
    I need to accept my past
    As well as let it go.
    I need to trust myself
    As well as us.
    Today.

Today I failed.
    But tomorrow is another day.
    Tomorrow I need to be stronger.
    I need to love myself
    As well as you.

THE INVITATION

you dance on the head of an angelic pin
    what music of earth compels you to spin
    i watch you and wonder with each measured stride
    what motivation, what reason, you so carefully hide
    dreams of what will be, dreams of what was
    these might entice you, if anything does
    we trace out the patterns, our paths come to cross
    i want to reach out, but am left at a loss
    what would I tell you, if my thoughts had a voice
    that you have such great power, that you have a choice
    live in this moment, this stitch of time
    breathe in the rapture you so carefully mime
    remove your grim mask at the masquerade ball
    remember this pin is mirrored, in spite of it all
    but you're afraid and mislead, confused and quite blind
    slowly and surely going out of your mind
    stop looking in faces and their widening gyres
    stop looking for answers in the flickering fires
    look within, dead angel, and know there is light
    beyond your numb thoughts, beyond your cold fright

i remain silent, lost in deep troubled thoughts
struggling to leave this cold cage that i've wrought
i dance near the edge of the angels' steel pin
and sometimes it feels i should finally give in
but the fringes whisper of miraculous things
should i step from this place, i may find i have wings
and so my dear friend, and angel in lace
see the trace of a smile upon my sweet face
will you jump with me into unknown darkness below
or stay in this hell that we already know

RANGE

They call my name,
    with the sound of tumbling rocks,
    wind through tunnels,
    cries of birds.

THE SNOW-CAPPED PEAKS
    with their stately dusted trees,
    steep cliffs of white,
    gently falling flakes.

AND SO I run to them,
    hair streaming in the wind,
    feet sliding on ice,
    breath a hazy mist.

THEY STAND AS ETERNAL MONUMENTS;
    giants tossing toy-sized boulders,

warriors standing tall;
sentries guarding secrets.

Y ET EACH ONE links to the next,
    holding hands in seamless rises,
    touching through hills,
    standing never alone.

SOLE DIVING

Someone lost their sole on the way to or from class.
    This is not a metaphor.
    It is no surprise that a heavily used walkway
    Between campus buildings and two apartment complexes
    Bears the varied signs of human passage
    Left by the slovenly, the misfortunate, the careless.
    Or the ones who, without gloves, would not dig in the snow
    That until recently lined this path in winter's colors.
    A gum wrapper, a drinking cup, a toothpick;
    The vestiges of lunch or breakfast quickly eaten and erased
    From between teeth before smiling at a cute classmate.
    A straw, a pen which was probably a good one once,
    But now lies muddied and cracked, ink bled into puddles.
    Lip balm, for that last minute gloss or protection against the cold.
    A paper clip scraped off papers shoved hastily out of the rain.
    These feel familiar in a trash-the-earth sort of way,
    Commonplace, hackneyed, the detritus of the common-folk.
    But the sole of a left shoe has a story to tell, if I could hear it.
    Was this the last straw on an already dreary grey Monday?
    Or barely a blip in the step of someone who did not notice

Because their step was so light and buoyant with joy
At the hint of spring, or a good grade, or a cancelled class.
Each day I wander toward my destination and back again.
Back and forth, day after day, I am musing about this one object.
It's just a heel, dusted and dirty, worn from this same path and others.
Were new shoes purchased that day amidst grumbling and sighs?
Or is that shoe still walking this path, tread slightly uneven,
Waiting for a sale or a paycheck or a ride to the store?
I forget that it is there until I see it again and start anew.
At least until I notice something else to make this walk fresh again.
Could I lose my sole and not notice? Could I nonchalantly recover?
This is most assuredly a metaphor.
Because, in the end, everything is if you look long enough.
And if you walk the same path too many times lost in thought.
Eyes searching past the grey ribbon of concrete.
To the possibilities behind, before, and all around,
Suddenly aware of your left shoe, the contents of your pockets
What you may have lost along the way, and your sole.

KAILEE

She's almost seven.
    Reading books about monkeys and bears
    Pointing to each word,
    Sounding out the long ones.
    Smiling at the pictures.
    She's just a few months shy of seven.
    Dressing in pink, giggling
    Trading stickers with her friends
    An infectious smile
    A shirt that says *I write my own story*
    She's very nearly seven.
    First grade and full of disease
    The scans were not good
    Pelvis, lungs, abdomen
    Fighting for her life.
    She's not even seven.

THE POET AS ARTIST

In 2010, performance artist Murina Abramovic created the largest performance art event in the history of the Museum of Modern Art in New York City. From March until May, she sat in a chair at a table and received visitors, gazing at each in immobile silence. In the end, she sat with 1,545 visitors for a total of 736 hours and 30 minutes. The man mentioned below is Ulay, a fellow artist of equal renown. I know little of their world and their story except what is recounted here.

SHE SAT, swathed in red fabric,
    Head bowed between moments,
    Long jet-black hair braided,
    Cascading down one shoulder.
    This is an unfamiliar world I am watching.
    Modern performance art
    Constantly re-defining itself
    Each piece demanding something more.

I FOUND her years later in a video posted online.

Social media telling a story
But only part of it.
And I didn't want to know more.
Complications and details would mar it.
I wanted that moment
To be only what it seemed
Though the cynic in me knew it wasn't.

SHE SAT at a table in the MOMA atrium
    Sitting, in turn, with strangers
    Who waited for hours
    Day after day, for three months.
    She would look at each one, unmoving
    The two would share silence
    And eye contact
    Until each passed the chair to the next.

BUT THE VIDEO I saw captured only one
    Of the hundreds who came
    To fill the hours and months
    Her head was bowed when he walked up
    To take his seat as the others had
    The lover she had not seen
    For over thirty years
    Each a muse to the other until it ended

HER EYES FILLED WITH TEARS, and his smiled
    He kept shaking his head
    As if there were no words
    She trembled, leaned forward, and reached for him
    He took her hands and whispered to her
    His heart finding voice

I could not hear him
But my heart knows what he said

I WONDERED briefly at the story waiting to be told,
    But I could not go find it,
    The poet was present
    This moment of beauty stronger than the truth
    And so my muse gazed at me in silence
    Until my mind wandered
    To consider the next person
    The one who sat in the chair when the ex-lover's turn ended.

LIMINAL

Between school shootings
    The children are still dying
    The bullets are still flying
    Blood still runs to the floor
    But we go silent about it
    Like it doesn't really count
    The echo of empathic dissonance

Schools should be safe spaces
    But repeatedly they are not
    Bullying becomes stark violence
    Hatred and toxic anger explode
    One victim becomes many
    Children cower under desks
    Sending a final text just in case

There is fear in my heart
    Like barbed wire incessant

The classroom still brings joy
Joy that still outweighs the fear
But what if it doesn't?
What if it comes here?
Could I take a bullet for them?

Would they ask me to?

MUSING

Muse, amuse me.
Inspire, expire, aspire,
desire.
Unknot the not,
know the no.
move the yes of yesterday to tomorrow
defy the cant of can't
move the canyon of can
closer than yon, can-did
Move it here
Adhere, cohere, sphere,
Sheer.
Speculate, concentrate,
emulate genius
us together, create, integrate,
escape
capable of Anything.

SILENCE

Find the silence
    Deep inside
    When anger fades
    And tears have dried
    Words can worsen
    Words can fail
    Endless speech
    To no avail
    An idle tongue
    An empty line
    Can say as much
    In half the time
    We must know quiet
    Must silence voice
    Listen closely
    When given choice
    Attend and hear
    But not to speak
    Empower, listen

Give no critique
Words have power
To peace have led
Sometimes the more
When left unsaid

EMPTY DOORWAYS
FOR TAMI

Many are just students - good, bad, strong, struggling.
    But some of them are thinkers and dreamers, thirsty.
    Drinking in all we can give, and seeking answers alone
    If we can't give them what they need.

T<small>HEY ARE OFTEN</small> tired and overloaded, stressed and nervous,
    Beyond that, they have walked many varied roads to get here.
    Each shares a passion for knowledge, wisdom, and skills
    Often just for the sake of having them.

A<small>ND</small>, oh do they challenge us and push us, make demands on us
    They question what we say, seeking clarity for the smallest confusions
    Yearning to succeed in everything, they take up all our time
    They seem relentless in their dedication.

A<small>ND THEN ONE DAY</small>, after a flurry of chaotic energy, they are gone

Like so many others, they are moving through and onward
Their time with us has ended, leaving our doorways standing empty
They seek greener pastures, different lives.

AND WHEN OUR new rosters come and we begin the cycle anew,
　We look for others like them, though it won't be quite the same,
　Because we know that for all their questions and all their fears
　They made us better than we were.

DAWN

Broken glass
    Shattered on the tile floor
    Smoky liquid seeping into the grout
    Trembling hand opens cupboard
    Another glass

Fire goes out
    The cigarette crushed
    Smoke swirling into the darkness
    Trembling hand creates light
    Another fire

Before Dawn
    Emptiness all around
    Lonely drifting into hazy sleep
    Trembling hand stills
    Broken dawn

. . .

VIOLENT WAKING
    Coughing breaks the silence
    Blood coats the walls floors couch bed
    Trembling hand reaches out
    Violent death

EYES CLOSE
    See cigarettes and blood
    Smoky memories fading into time
    Trembling hand covers face
    Eyes weep

HELL HATH NO FURY

I am a woman.
    I say this with declaration, certainty.
    Pride, even.
    But if I were to be honest,
    (because there is truth in poetry)
    I don't know what that means.

IN THE MINEFIELD OF STEREOTYPES,
    It becomes half simple.
    I cry too often, care too deeply.
    I like books, cats, baby animals.
    I worry too much about my weight.
    Sometimes I'm afraid of the dark.

BUT THEN IT COMPLICATES,
    Or I become more complicated.
    Which is also feminine, I suppose.
    I'm not sure which is true,

(If there is truth even in poetry)
But either way, I stop fitting.

I AM CHILDLESS.
    I find them adorable, but creepy.
    Huge eyes and needs,
    Too unsure to provide for another
    I have no maternal gene
    And feel no pang to create.

I REJECTED MY CURVES.
    And met eyeroll and disbelief
    As if those curves defined me.
    No thought as to why I would,
    Just the unspoken suggestion
    That I am now less of a woman.

I AM A SUCCESS.
    I out-earn my spouse (whatever that's worth),
    With more education behind me,
    But only for the simplest of reasons.
    I thought I would need to be.
    At least it's English, that's woman.

I AM NATURAL SKINNED.
    I like my face the way it is,
    Though if truth be told (since this is poetry),
    I mostly cannot be bothered,
    Goddess has given me one face,
    I do not make myself another.

          . . .

I AM A SQUARE PEG.
>   Video games aren't made for me,
>   But I play them.
>   Fantasy fiction is not written for me,
>   But I read it.
>   I dance in circles made for the hunters.

I AM MYSELF.
>   Think and build with me,
>   Call me lovely, call me strange,
>   But take me for who I am,
>   For this is poetry, and, so, truth.
>   I am a woman.

I AM, I GUESS

I am broken.
    I know I look and sound fine,
    (In a general sense, not an aesthetic one)
    But I'm not. Fairly sure I never will be.
    All the pills, the chiropractor, the doctors,
    The injections, the slight shrug of the shoulders
    Because they don't know.
    Neither do I.

I AM ALICE.
    One pill makes me tired,
    One pill makes me dizzy,
    I don't know what the third one does,
    But I take it anyway.
    Morning, midday, dinnertime, bedtime.
    Regimented as much as you can regiment a poet.
    I forget sometimes.

        . . .

I am tired.
> (I mean, in some ways we all are
> Because life is relentless even when it's good).
> Chronic pain is exhausting, chronic fatigue is, too.
> Though, I suppose that is only logical
> Sometimes, I don't make sense,
> Or I simply can't make sense,
> I confuse myself.

I am angry.
> But really too damn tired to do anything
> Except grumble at people now and then.
> It isn't fair…but, honestly, what is?
> It is what it is and here I am
> I don't know what I am, but I will keep being it
> I'm in it too far to give up now,
> I am not defeated.

I am alive.
> And that's really the important thing,
> Isn't it? Being alive means love
> Pain can be blocked out, ignored
> Stuffed away for awhile to make space
> Space for deep breaths and laughter and joy
> A life full of all the things that make a good life good
> I am life.

ROMANTICIZING
FOR BRIANNA

Jagged, raised flesh
    Thin lines criss-crossed
    Pale white, deep red
    Healed and then made again
    Always made again

A DIFFERENT KIND of art
    My skin weeps for me
    Tragically beautiful

ROLLED down sleeves
    Hide the shame, anguish
    Scabs itch and pull and ooze
    And the pain remains
    Always remains

        . . .

I'd love to find a boy
   To kiss these scars
   Artistically tortured

Teeth rotting, acid burns
   Throat inflamed, voice broken
   Swollen cheeks, bloodshot eyes
   And every meal is one too many
   Always one too many.

So strong to be so thin
   Pretty girls don't eat
   Brokenly romantic

Hair falling out, nails thinning
   Brittle bones pushing through
   Blotchy yellow skin, confusion
   Seizures fainting and always cold
   Always feeling cold.

Jealous of your self-control
   No stars without darkness
   Poetically damaged

Strip the lies, no beauty left
   Ugly, dark, violent, devastating
   No escape, no release, no joy
   Always trying to drown the demons
   Always they can breathe

             . . .

S*UICIDES ARE JUST ANGELS*
 who want to go home
 Perfectly deceased

S*top.*

A FLEETING DARKNESS

Her idle fingers make designs with the crumbs,
    With movements unfocused, mindless, wooden.
    He sits at the table with her, feeling like a suspect.
    He licks his lips, still tasting the bitter chocolate,
    His own fingers curling around a mug barely warm,
    The room still filled with the scent of evergreen.

HE GLANCES out the window at the evergreen
    As still she draws idle pictures with the crumbs
    He feels a chill and once more wishes it were warm
    Standing, he moves towards her, his legs wooden,
    She hasn't even touched her hot chocolate,
    It sits in the center of the table looking suspect.

A SHARP SOUND, a woodpecker the likely suspect
    Rustling outside amongst the boughs of evergreen
    He takes a sip from his mug, the tepid taste of chocolate
    Washing his mouth free of the last few crumbs

His hand rubs across his face, unshaven, feeling wooden,
He then drops his hand to her shoulder, tense and warm

It amuses him that he is cold and she is warm
    His heart leaps in his chest, she is suspect
    Her chair creaks as she shifts, the sound wooden,
    As the woodpecker still dances in the evergreen,
    The table decorated in lines made of idle crumbs,
    The room smelling more of pine than chocolate

He softly offers to heat her cooled hot chocolate,
    She looks up at him and smiles, her eyes warm.
    For the moment, her hands have forgotten the crumbs,
    There is a love in her face, he hopes he is suspect
    A lasting depth is in her eyes like winter evergreen
    He squeezes her shoulder, no longer feeling wooden

The woodpecker plays its song, hollow and wooden,
    As he gathers up the mugs of now cold hot chocolate
    While they heat, he feeds the fire a branch of evergreen
    And soon the mugs are steaming and the kitchen warm
    He says casually it'll be a beautiful day, I suspect
    She drinks with fingers curled, having forgotten the crumbs

She sweeps the crumbs away with movements not wooden
    The dark memory, the suspect, drowned in hot chocolate
    And hand in warm hand, they walk among the evergreen.

AS I LAY DREAMING

My eyes are closed as I write this,
    there's nothing to see but my own words
    as they unfold in tiny black letters on a blank screen.
    I know what words they are,
    And the blackness behind my eyelids
    Is darker, warmer, deeper, and more full

I DON'T NEED to see them birthed,
    My mind has already given them life
    Or, rather, the muse has already whispered them to me.
    I am merely transcribing them,
    Her voice in my head brings me solace
    When the solitary night seems too heavy on my head

TO SPEAK in silence without looking,
    Is an exercise in faith and trust, because I know
    I know that the words are growing with each keystroke,
    But still I find myself cheating,

Eyes sliding open to see if it is all real
Or if I'm only dreaming that my fingers strike true.

SOMETIMES, they write nonsense,
    Like some child's secret language, hidden
    Except I am no child and I have forgotten the code,
    So the gibberish is erased,
    With the hope that the muse will repeat
    The sacred lines of the song my soul is singing.

I AM TIRED, but the words will come,
    Because if I close my eyes without them
    I will only lie in swirling thought and not in sleep.
    In this way, the swirls subside,
    And I find that I can set aside the song
    For a little while, to rest my fingers and the muse.

AND IN THAT darkness just before sleep,
    I learn a sacred truth that whispers to me
    Calliope singing, if only I could hear her laughter
    As I fall back on my eyes to see,
    When she knows that if I keep the faith,
    I'll find my way to a deep abiding truth

A THOUSAND VOICES have spoken it
    That if we can let go of our need to see
    The ocean of things that do not need to be seen
    We would know deeply of love
    And in that moment of enlightenment
    If we could but touch it, would be our bliss

          . . .

But sleep comes upon me now,
>   Despite my longing to touch the moment
>   Despite my need to achieve perfect understanding
>   That dances just beyond reach
>   The strains of Calliope's song resonate
>   with flawless clarity....as I lay dreaming...

A WOLF IN HANNAH'S CLOTHING

Trapped in a body
    Made for someone else
    It radiates out into
    Every part of your life
    Your name is wrong
    Your voice is wrong
    Your clothes are wrong
    The pronouns are wrong
    Few understand, few want to
    Alone in a crowded room
    Too many identities
    Crammed into one

TRAPPED in a label
    Created by someone else
    Binary questions polarizing
    Are you gay or straight
    As if it was only about sex
    As if it was only about body

As if it was only about attraction
She doesn't understand,
He doesn't want to
Too much loneliness
Only in the dark do you forget
Light and mirrors and people
Remind you of who you aren't

Trapped in a mind
    That wants to be someone else
    Feeling brave, you try to pass,
    But too often passed over
    You bind, you medicate
    You therapy, you rant
    You dream, you cry
    All you want is to be you
    The you that lives inside
    And yearns to be reborn
    Rechristened by flame
    Like a phoenix from the ash.

BESSIE

Bessie done cut her old man, a neighbor reported
   When she returned home from church,
   And heard the gossip spreading like fire.
   It was two hours after the knife struck home.

JUST AFTER MIDNIGHT, on a cold Louisiana night,
   A man lay still on a New Orleans sidewalk.
   The evening of their final battle had ended
   With him hemorrhaging into shock and death.

HE HAD OFTEN BEAT BESSIE, they said,
   Run her into the street three or four times a month.
   But this time he crossed a dangerous line,
   Erasing seven years of common-law marriage.

HIS FATAL ANNOUNCEMENT was simply this:
   He didn't care much for Bessie's daughter.

If you don't like Dorothy, she said,
It's best that you and me part. He exploded.

YOUNGER-THAN-TEN JOSEPH FLED with his sisters,
    Pleading with the neighbors; his cries full of fear.
    My Papa's beating my Mamma, he told them,
    Said he was going to kill us all.

BESSIE DID NOT DENY what she had done,
    As he stumbled out onto the sidewalk and collapsed.
    I run to the armoire and got a large knife, she said,
    And when he come to hit me again, I stabbed him.

DIAGNOSE, analyze, study, and dissect.
    Explore race, common-law marriage, homicide.
    Study the streets of New Orleans, 1925-1945,
    Sit at a desk at university and write.

ASK countless questions of why and how,
    But is it really more complicated than this:
    He was a mean man to his wife, the neighbor stated,
    And...she is a good smart Woman.

DACHAU, DECEMBER 1995

the concertina wire is still there
    after all these years it coils relentlessly
    tightening a boundary around us as it did them
    steel edges against a sullen grey sky
    I doubt if even the sun could make them shine
    wire and guard towers are the first things I see of this place

ONCE INSIDE THIS angry border I am struck
    by the emptiness of it and the deceptive openness
    I find it strange that what had been destroyed
    has since been reconstructed for the future
    a disarmingly empty and barren replica
    of where I can't imagine so many tried to live

THE OTHERS ARE only skeletons arranged on the ground
    neatly in rows with space enough to walk between
    making the irony weigh heavy in my mind
    as heavy as the realization that these buildings

    are shaped like the boxcars that carried people here
    and turned them into ghosts

I LIGHTEN my coat against a day that is so cold
    as the snow swirls softly in a bitter wind
    that whistles through the trees that hid this place
    from the world I hug my arms and walk
    I think I feel the thin shifts that covered other bodies
    bodies with haunted eyes and foreign names

I CAME to this place with someone who did not
    have the strength to see what I am seeing
    turned away and preferring to stay lost
    in sheltered memories of home across the sea
    memories that allow forgetting I cannot do this
    I must answer the urge to re member them

I WALK without my country and silent voices speak
    they tell stories through stark photos that rip and tear at me
    through words written in a language I cannot read
    through empty rooms and empty ovens of charred brick
    where someone finally found a freedom

CRAZY WOMEN

I have been thinking about crazy women.
    Embroiled in a hectic life of my own,
    It fits in a crazy way.

BUT I DON'T THINK I am these crazy women
    Who are dancing through this mindful chaos
    Then again..perhaps...

SOMETIMES, I don't know where I'm dancing.
    Maybe with the late Mrs. Rochester,
    Or Miss Havisham.

BECAUSE THEY DON'T SEEM to be the crazy women
    Dancing through my head either, but I don't know.
    It's 3 am.

            . . .

And then it occurs to me that we are all the same,
    A maelstrom of crazy women in wild attics,
    It's a crazy world, it is.

A crazy world where we have trouble acting normal,
    But we will be loved even as we talk to angels
    We're beautiful wrecks, round here.

We take a swing, but don't mean to harm
    Sometimes we go full speed ahead
    In the wrong direction.

Yes, it's 3 am and drops of Jupiter are in
    our eyes and we do not want to be
    The queen, we scream.

But out here, it is not stuck at three or any hour,
    Days will come dawn by dawn and I will see
    The morning star.

And go through each day with songs in my head
    Music that tells stories in rhythm and verse
    Though with deeper voices.

They have a presence that dances through my soul
    And they knit the fabric of their own stories
    In sacred silence.

. . .

AND THESE WOMEN, my sisters, they speak to me
   With voices that defy traditional confinement.
   As does mine.

THEY REFUSE to be understood by the rules of man,
   But in spite, or because of, this, they demand love.
   As do I.

SO LOVE these crazy women in a crazier world,
   Stay up very, very late; let hopeful eyes meet the sunrise.
   Stay with me.

REFERENCES:
   "She Will be Loved" – Maroon 5
   "She Talks to Angels" – Black Crowes
   "Beautiful Wreck" – Shawn Mullins
   "Her Eyes" – Pat Monahan
   "3am" – Matchbox 20
   "Meet Virginia" – Train
   "Drops of Jupiter" – Train
   "Mary Jane" – Alanis Morrisette
   "Round Here" – Counting Crows

I AM A FEMINIST

I am a feminist ...

...because I like to paint my nails and then go target shooting when they dry.

...because choosing not to be a mother doesn't make me less of a woman.

...and neither does breast reduction.

I am a feminist ...

...because moms who don't work and working moms should be valued equally.

...because a man can be a stay at home dad and paint his daughter's nails

...but he's not babysitting his own kids.

I am a feminist ...

...because crying like a little girl sounds exactly the same as crying like a little boy

...because 'you throw like a girl' is just as stupid and insulting as being told to 'man up'

...and I don't feel like smiling.

I am a feminist ...

...because the armor women wear in popular culture does not

protect their vital organs.

...because strong women aren't always lesbians, sensitive men aren't always gay

...and I don't care if they are.

I am a feminist ...

... because birth control should be accessible to men and women without judgment

...because making abortions illegal will only stop safe abortions.

...and genital mutilation still exists

I am a feminist ...

...because body parts should not determine privilege, opportunities, and rights.

...because women make up half the population but are grossly under-represented

...in issues that involve them.

I am a feminist ....

...because we don't worry enough about women feeding babies in the bathroom

...because we worry too much about the genitals of everyone else in the bathroom

...and it has nothing to do with bathrooms

I am a feminist ...

...because cat-calling is not harmless and 'it was just locker room talk' is not an excuse.

...because I am terrified of walking alone in an unfamiliar place at night

...and in broad daylight.

I am a feminist ...

...because alcohol should not be used to excuse the rapist or blame the victim

...because domestic violence and sexual assault happen regardless of gender

...and both are underreported.

I am a feminist ...

...because we should not blame victims for crimes perpetrated against them.

...because one in every three women will be sexually assaulted in her lifetime.

...and we have no idea how many men.

I am a feminist ...

...because we live in a rape culture and yet many do not even know what that means

...because all men should not pay for the behavior of rapists and misogynists.

...but the rapist should

I am a feminist ...

...because the first response to 'women's rights' shouldn't be 'so I can hit women?'

...because women are not vending machines to put friendship in until sex falls out.

...this is rape culture.

I am a feminist ...

...because gender inequality hurts all genders, of which there are more than two

...because we all deserve dignity and respect regardless of what gender we are or aren't

...and I am human

BLOSSOMS

There are no words in answer, to capture how we feel,
    But I see your softly broken heart that cannot really heal.
    I do not claim to understand; I will never really know
    But your love, your heart, your heartache cannot help but show.
    I leave a flower now and then, a bloom that's bright and fair,
    Its color soon to fade on stone, but no less is my care.
    I don't wonder when you'll see, don't watch for your reply,
    I do it for the little boy to whom you said goodbye.
    I did not know you on that day to hold you as you cried.
    And now the lamb upon his stone draws me to his side.
    The sun will warm his stone by day, the moon shines in the night,
    And I, too, watch over him, with my flawed and human sight.
    A promise made many months ago I've never really spoken.
    That I would not let him go for as long as heart stayed broken.
    Even now a new day dawns, and a little girl will come and play,
    She will heal your loving heart, though broken it will stay.
    And I will gather double blossoms, blooms so bright and fair,
    Some for stone and some for crowns to place upon her hair.
    And you will tell her stories so she will come to know her brother,
    And I will tell her stories of the golden heart that is her mother.

JUST MOVING

We all know tired.
    Going on because we must,
    Doing because we can't not do.
    The stress, the exhaustion, the need,
    All roll together until we are just moving.

THEN THE MOMENT COMES.
    We finish the race, complete the task.
    Minutes filled with plans and things put off.
    But first we collapse into a restful place to dream.
    Dream, recover, rejuvenate, reborn, reboot, reinvigorate.

I AM NOT YET THERE.
    I am still tired, still driven.
    Still working and eyeing the grindstone.
    But I know, oh I know, that I will get there.
    I, too, will find that restful sleep of infinite rebirth.

. . .

I just need to get there.
    I will go on because I must,
    I will do because I can't not do.
    Stressed and exhausted with need,
    All rolled together until I am just moving.

Just moving.

JUST STUDENTS

Many I meet are just students,
    Good, bad, strong, struggling.
    To them I am just a teacher
    Hard, fun, crazy, good, tough

BUT SOME OF them are learners
    Drinking all we can give
    If the teachers fail them
    They read, talk, push, think.

ALL WALKS OF LIFE, all kinds,
    They share a thirst, a passion
    Knowledge, wisdom, skills
    Often just to have them.

THEY CHALLENGE US, push us
    Make us better than we are

SECONDHAND MEMORIES, AUGUST 11, 1995

You were lucky, they tell me, shocked.
    They can't believe that I survived.
I look at the photos of the car blankly
    and just shake my head;
        Perhaps trying to erase the dense fog.
    But it stays.
All I can do is once again regurgitate
    the hard, cold facts.
And I'm tired of that, I've done it so often,
    I have nothing more to say.

How can I respond to something that was me,
    but feels more like a story on the news?
Then I shift my weight, and the pain reels back,
    And I know.
I know I was the trapped victim,
    Sirens, whirling lights and a crowd for me.
I know it was my family that looked on

    as trapped seconds stretched to minutes stretched to more...

I never lost consciousness, they tell me.
  But a policeman kept telling me his name.
    How did my forgetting make him feel?
I became slowly aware of hospital lights,
  starched sheets, thick smells, people.
    Faces drifting.
X-rays, CAT scans, they keep moving me from room to room.
  It hurts, but they won't stop,
    It will never stop...

Hand on the Bible, I swear the oath,
  To tell the truth, the whole truth, so help me, God.
I just echo myself as 28 pairs of eyes watch.
  I don't remember, I don't remember,
  I don't remember...
The bustling attorney pries out the same answer,
  regardless of what questions he asks,
    I cannot remember.

No flashbacks inspires by those stark photos
  of twisted metal and broken glass;
No memories return when paramedics,
  police officers, witnesses, tell me what they saw,
    what I said, what I did;
Nothing triggered by the pain, by the black
  skid marks scarring the road drenched in summer sunset
    Nothing.

And then there's him...what do I say of him?
  He's a faceless name, for why would I remember him
    and nothing else?
He stumbled from his empty car, slurring a lie.

Blood ran from his nose as he claimed it wasn't him.
    A witness tasted fury and was restrained.
Events, commotion, chaos whiled around me.
    I was there…and yet not there…

Six times he stumbled and was freed to stumble again,
    His seventh is the one that punched my life
        Even this time the cuffs fell open and he walked away.
He offered up his plea, and someone listened,
    A lawyer who knew people who knew people.
        Though he has been disbarred and must seek help.
Who is offering to help me? Can I trust the system
    to protect me, when the same system lets them go?
        It is not enough and the forgetting is too much.

I wonder if he thinks of it or if the demons are solely mine.
    He comes to my mind more than I'd like.
I wonder why he chose to include me in his loss of control
    And then erase it carelessly from my mind.
Over and over I ask why he was given this amazing power
        to blur my memory and change my life in just a few seconds,
        doing *at least fifty miles an hour.*
        Even the police report sounds angry.

Time has passed, the way it always does.
    I like to think I've let go,
        But it stays with me every day.
            I wonder if I can ever really move on,
    making progress in darkness, with eyes the do not grow accustomed.
I can see nothing of that day…but do I want to see his face in my dreams?
    Do I want to remember?

Undecided, I sit and wait
Cradling my second-hand memories and wondering if they will ever be mine.

THE TEST OF THE WINE TASTER

Swirling the contents of the goblet, she inhaled deeply, then drank. "It is indeed unique to the palette. The fragrance is sharp and sweet; a strong bouquet with a hint of spice. Its hue is darker than most reds and somber, contrasting with the full-bodied taste. It has the freshness of a young vintage, but the dignity of age. It is unlike any I've known, and yet seems strangely familiar. I cannot place the label, origin, or year." She smiled her defeat and he grinned, sharp teeth glistening. She gasped.

THE LOGOPHILE

Countless words
    We meet each day
    They float to ear
    Then drift away
    Stop to listen
    And you will find
    They'll touch your heart
    Expand your mind
    Such power born
    In word and phrase
    Can bring a depth
    To random days
    In this world
    Of text and speed
    To plant a word
    Is to plant a seed
    Give it life
    Germination
    Let it spread
    Cultivation

Mind to lips
In exultation
The living words
In jubilation
Words in beauty
Never lose
Let the language
Be your muse

TRYING NOT TO DWELL

A shadowy presence in my mind, lurking
    Blotted out most of the time when I'm occupied
    Time with friends, errands to run, chores to do
    But then, under the glow of a supermoon
    And the quiet hum of tires on the ethereal highway,
    It comes back to me in a wave of melancholy
    It does that sometimes, less often than the pain
    Sometimes it comes as anger, but not tonight
    Tonight it came out of nowhere dressed in sadness
    Like a shadow in the night, a cloud in the sky

IT CAME and I was reminded not just that I hurt
    But it softly reminded me how and why I am broken
    Not in a way that stops me from loving life
    Not in a way that shatters dreams or saps hope
    Not in a way that leaves me crippled and lost
    But just a little less than whole, a little bit flawed
    Just little broken like a chip in a glass figurine
    A rough edge that time smoothed out but did not erase

. . .

THIS TIME it comes to me in numbers that prick my eyes
    And roll through my mind like an insidious code
    The 11th day of the 8th month
    The 38th minute of the sixth hour after noon.
    The temperature was 78 degrees.
    His speed was over 50, mine was less than 5
    A quarter percent of his blood was alcohol.
    It was the tenth day after I bought the car
    The first car I'd ever owned
    The third month I'd had my license.
    Now I spend forty dollars to have my bones cracked
    Hoping it will hold for four weeks until I return
    I had five shots driven into my spine for no relief.
    I was twenty three and it has now been 19 years
    I cannot remember and I cannot forget

BUT DON'T MOURN for me – the shadow will pass
    The chip will remain, but I'm not really broken
    When I smile I mean it, when I laugh I feel it
    The moon is beautiful tonight and I am alive.
    Alive.

FENESTRA

Turning cards with graceful hands
    Revealing scenes of fantastic lands
    Thoughtful eyes on thoughtful face
    As each card laid in proper place
    A half a smile, a tilted head
    She speaks although no words are said
    I watch her in this sacred task
    And wonder at her missing mask
    Her face alight with mind and heart
    As she finds the meaning in the art

WE HEAR the timbre of voice again
    With cards laid out, tableaux of ten
    She taps each one with shapely nail
    And brings to life each carven tale
    Empress, cup, sword, and knight
    She walks us through her gift of sight
    Hands alive with earthen spells

I listen to the tale she tells
The cards are gorgeous and so is she
A goddess she shall ever be

WORLD OF MEANING

Worlds of meaning
    Oscillating in space
    Resonating outward
    Dancing back
    Sound meets meaning
    Bridging rivers
    Reaching out
    Experiencing affinity
    All from voice
    Tossed to the air
    Holding on; letting go
    Exploring connections
    Lifting barriers
    Invisible but present
    Felt and heard
    Existence confirmed

ABOUT THE AUTHOR

"Dr. Merrill has lived in Western New York for her entire life. She grew up in Bloomfield and Honeoye Falls and the headed up to SUNY Potsdam to get her Bachelor's Degree in Secondary Education and English. She then went downstate to get her Masters and Doctorate at SUNY Binghamton. She started teaching at Finger Lakes Community College in 2004 and is now Professor of English and Director of Honors Studies.

She is fascinated by the influence of popular culture and the subconscious power of mythology and ancient stories. Her teaching reflects a wide range of pedagogical interests such as Harry Potter, JRR Tolkien, Alice in Wonderland, and Women Who Kill along with courses in writing and literature.

She currently lives in Canandaigua with her husband of over ten years and their three cats. When not doing FLCC work, she enjoys doing jigsaw puzzles, hiking, reading, drawing, writing, spending time with her family, and officiating the occasional wedding."

www.ingramcontent.com/pod-product-compliance
Lightning Source LLC
Chambersburg PA
CBHW061335040426
42444CB00011B/2935